T0197501

You are GOLDEN!

KELLY KAINER BILLINGTON

There are so many colors we can see that shine brightly for you and me!

In America,
we are free
and so happy to be
in God's country!

*There is another color
for you and me
That we may not
be able to see!*

But as God's children, it is no surprise that we are indeed GOLDEN in His eyes!

As we follow our heart
because it never lies
we live by the GOLDEN Rule,
which is so wise!

When I want good things to happen to me,

I am good to people and animals too, you see!

Because, what we give is what we receive!

That is how it works for you and me!

*And when we give to others
peace, happiness, and love,*

We have made them happy
and God smiles on
us from above!

So be GOLDEN,
in the way you treat others
and in all you do!

For the GOLDEN Rule
simply says:

Do unto others as you would have them do unto you.

Luke 6:31

That way,
we will all live happily
in America
or wherever you may be,

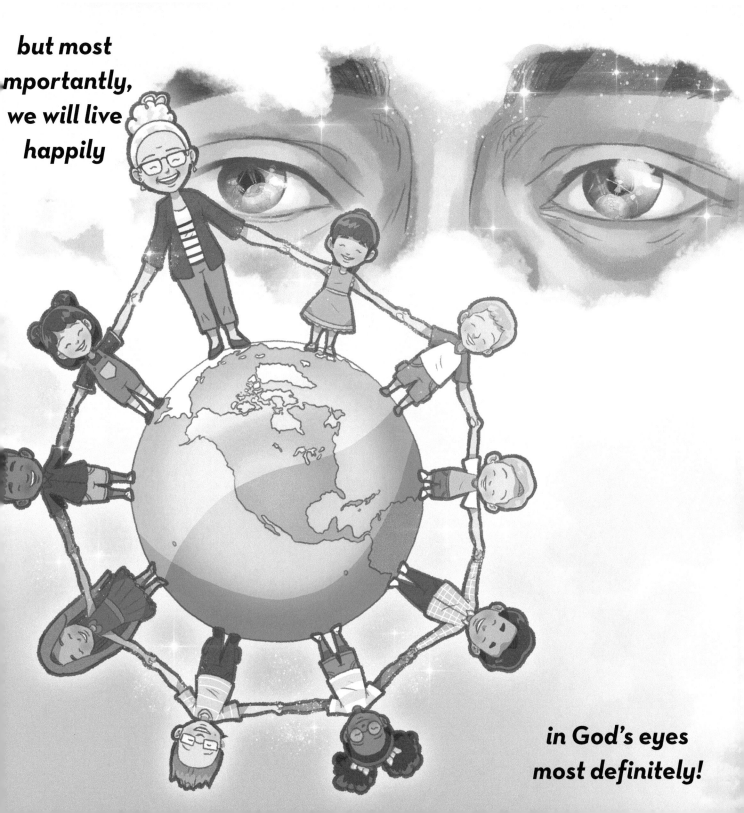

but most importantly, we will live happily

in God's eyes most definitely!

I LOVINGLY DEDICATE
THIS BOOK TO

MY MOTHER,
MY SON,
AND MY GRANDSONS!

Thank you Mother for teaching me right from wrong
And for being such a wonderful example in Christ!
May God bless you and keep you in your heavenly place!

Thank you Son for being such a wonderful Son, Husband, and Father!
You have a heart of gold!
And you will forever hold a special place in my heart!
Love you always!

Thank you to both of my Grandsons for being such a blessing in my life!
You both are the best! And I am such a lucky Nana!
I love you both to the moon and back always and forever!

I am so grateful to God for my blessings
as all glory always goes to Him!

May He bless you and keep you!
May He make His face shine upon you
and give you His grace!

ABOUT THE AUTHOR

Kelly Kainer Billington was born and raised in Southeast Texas. She is a lovingly devoted wife, mother, and grandmother (Nana), and she advocates that her family and God are most important to her.

She earned her Bachelor of Science degree in Business Administration-Management w/Teacher Certification. After 12 years in public schools, she felt a calling to enter the real estate world. She became a broker, investor, and renovator and manages the family businesses.

She authors and creates her own website at www.kellykainerbillington.com. And she has included a beautiful tribute to her beloved Mother on her JOY Comes in the Morning web page. She created this page to honor her Mother whose middle name was JOY, and to honor her courageous battle with Alzheimer's. Kelly has written and copyrighted a documentary in regard to their experiences and discoveries of the Alzheimer's disease. She is sharing it on her website in hopes that it will help someone. She knows her Mother would be sporting that infamous MiMi smile if it were to help just one person! That is the kind of person she was! Simply Beautiful!

Kelly has written another children's book titled, God's Goodness in You and Me, which focuses on bringing God back to the forefront! She is also the author of the up and coming NANA and ME Series! This series focuses on topics like the Golden Rule, Honesty is the Best Policy, Cleanliness is next to Godliness, etc...

As Kelly continues to move forward in her career as an author, she hopes to help and inspire people of all ages with her publications!

NOTES

WestBow Press books may be ordered through booksellers or by contacting:

WestBow Press
A Division of Thomas Nelson & Zondervan
1663 Liberty Drive
Bloomington, IN 47403
www.westbowpress.com
844-714-3454

Scripture taken from the NEW AMERICAN STANDARD BIBLE®, Copyright © 1960, 1962, 1963, 1968, 1971, 1972, 1973, 1975, 1977, 1995 by The Lockman Foundation. Used by permission. www.Lockman.org

ISBN: 978-1-6642-3686-8 (sc)
ISBN: 978-1-6642-3687-5 (e)

Library of Congress Control Number: 2021911681

Print information available on the last page.

WestBow Press rev. date: 12/29/2021

WESTBOW
PRESS®
A DIVISION OF THOMAS NELSON
& ZONDERVAN

Printed in the United States
by Baker & Taylor Publisher Services